LEARN, DRAW & COLOR
Ocean Creatures

LEARN, DRAW & COLOR
Ocean Creatures

Discover 26 of the Most Fascinating Ocean Creatures on the Planet!

Happy Fox
BOOKS

Welcome

Discover 26 of the most fascinating animals on the planet!

Learn all about where they live, what makes them so unique, and how they go about their everyday lives. Impress your friends with fun facts—for example, did you know that the male seahorse carries the babies?!

You'll also learn how to draw each creature in just a few simple steps. Plus, there are 26 full-page pictures for you to color in.

Have fun!

COLORING TOOLS

Using whatever medium you like, bring these delightful animal designs to life! Different coloring tools can create super cool effects and moods to an illustration—for example, markers make more a vibrant statement, while colored pencils are easy to blend and offer a softer feel. Have fun experimenting with some of these mediums:

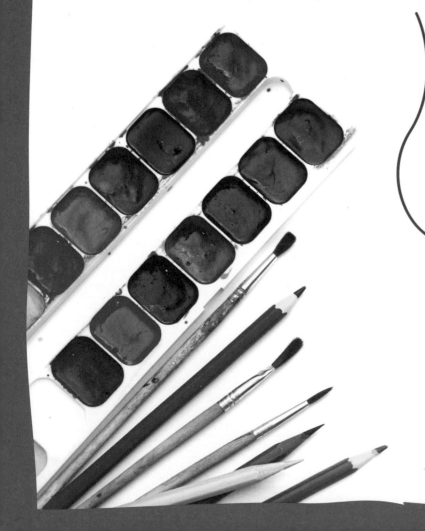

- **Markers**
- **Colored pencils**
- **Colored pens**
- **Gel pens**
- **Watercolors**
- **Crayons**

COLOR THEORY

With color, illustrations take on a life of their own. Remember: when it comes to painting and coloring, there are no rules. The most fun part is to play with color, relax, and enjoy the process and the beautiful, finished result. Feel free to mix and match colors and tones. Work your way from primary colors to secondary colors to tertiary colors, combining different tones to create all kinds of different effects. If you aren't familiar with color theory, here is a quick, easy guide to the basic colors and combinations you will be able to create.

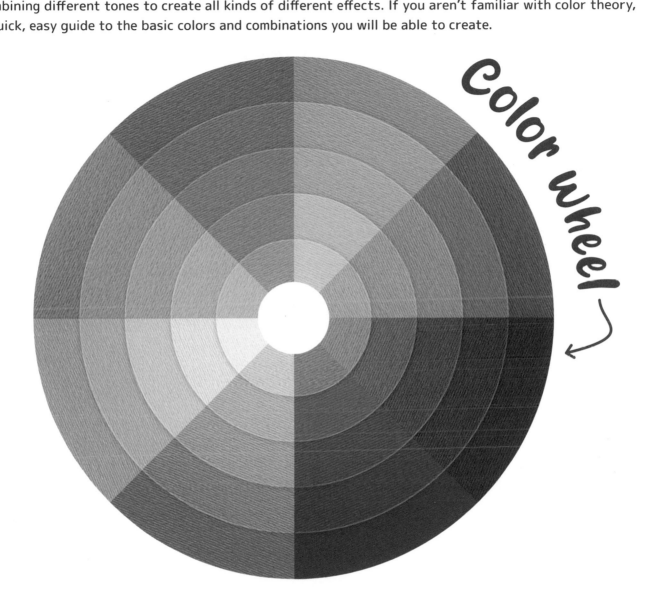

Color wheel

Primary colors:

These are the colors that cannot be obtained by mixing any other colors; they are yellow, blue, and red.

Secondary colors:

These colors are obtained by mixing two primary colors in equal parts; they are green, purple, and orange.

Tertiary colors:

These colors are obtained by mixing one primary color and one secondary color.

Cont

ents

BOTTLENOSE DOLPHIN

MEET THE OCEAN'S BUBBLE-BLOWING ACROBAT

These sociable marine mammals are known for their friendly and playful nature. They surf on waves and even blow bubbles to help catch their prey! They have been seen releasing bubble nets at schools of fish to confuse and trap them or to herd them to the surface. Bottlenose dolphins hunt using sound and echoes, also called echolocation. This is when they make clicking sounds that vibrate through the water and bounce back off objects, enabling them to discover how far away their prey is by measuring how long it takes the vibrations to come back to them. They can make up to 1,000 clicks per second! These charismatic creatures communicate with squeaks and whistles, which can be used to identify them.

©Mike Hill/Getty

? Did you know...
They're incredible acrobats and can jump up to 16 ft out of the water.

Fun Fact
These super swimmers can move at speeds of over 18 mph.

Bottlenose dolphins must surface to breathe through their blowhole; they can hold their breath for up to seven minutes.

COMMON BOTTLENOSE DOLPHIN
FACT FILE

CLASS
MAMMAL

GROUP NAME
POD

TERRITORY
TROPICAL AND TEMPERATE WATERS WORLDWIDE

HOW BIG!

AVERAGE LIFE SPAN
40—60 YEARS

DIET
CARNIVORE
FISH, SQUID, AND CRUSTACEANS

They may look like they're smiling, but this is just the natural curve of their mouths.

Did you know...
? They travel together in pods, usually groups of up to 30 dolphins, and occasionally super pods of up to 1,000.

BRAINY FISH

Bottlenose dolphins are super intelligent. Their brain-to-body ratio is the second-biggest after humans. They are one of the few animals that can recognize themselves in mirrors and have learned to use tools.

How to draw... a dolphin

1. SMALL ARCH: Start by drawing a shape like the one above. This will be the dolphin's body.

2. MOUTH AND TAIL: Add a little snout on the right, and a big flipper tail on the left of the shape.

You can use an eraser to rub out the original line so it creates one continuous shape

3. FACE: Draw a smile and a little eye.

4. FINS: Start by drawing the top fin in the middle of the dolphin's back. Then in line with its eye, draw the side fin..

Erase the original line

5. BELLY: Following the line of the body underneath, create a tummy.

6. COLOR! Why not choose a few different blues to give your dolphin some texture?

LOBSTER

GET YOUR CLAWS INTO THESE LOBSTER MYTHS

Did you know that lobsters aren't actually red? That's just the color they turn when they're cooked. And it's a myth that they scream when boiled. This would actually be impossible, as lobsters don't have vocal chords. There are two main types of lobster: the spiny lobster, with its large antennae, and the more familiar "true" lobster, which has smaller antennae and large pincer claws. True lobsters usually have two pincers: a crusher and a cutter, but they don't have to worry if they lose one, as they can grow a new claw if needed. Another myth is that lobsters mate for life. The dominant male mates with a female for about two weeks before moving on to the next.

©RLSPHOTO/Getty

©RLSPHOTO/Getty

Lobsters don't chew their food in their mouths; their teeth are found in one of their two stomachs.

Did you know...
A lobster's claw can exert a pressure of up to 100 pounds per square inch.

Lobsters have clear blood, but it turns blue when it hits the air.

Fun Fact

They can swim forwards and backwards, but they'll go into reverse if alarmed.

AMERICAN LOBSTER

FACT FILE

CLASS
INVERTEBRATE

GROUP NAME
RISK

TERRITORY
NORTHWEST ATLANTIC OCEAN

AVERAGE LIFE SPAN
UP TO 100 YEARS

DIET
OMNIVORE
FISH, SMALL CRUSTACEANS, AND MOLLUSCS

HOW BIG!

Did you know...

Lobsters have poor eyesight; they use their antennae to smell and their legs to taste.

WHEN NATURE CALLS

These crustaceans have a strange way of talking to each other. They don't have vocal chords; instead, they release urine from just under their eyes to communicate with other lobsters, whether it's with their mate or during a fight.

How to draw... a lobster

1. BODY: Start with an upside down teardrop shape like this.

2. SNIP, SNIP: Draw a claw on either side of the head.

3. LEGS AND TAIL: Add some little legs at the bottom of the body and a heart-shaped tail.

4. EYES ON STICKS: At the top of the head, draw two sticks with circles on the end. Add a black pupil inside each eye. Then draw two curly whiskers next to each eye.

5. EXTRA LEGS: Draw six extra legs (three on each side of the body) and add a cute little smile.

6. Stripy! Use orange, brown, and red to color your lobster to create its armored shell.

SEAL

THESE BELLY-FLOPPING MAMMALS GET OUR SEAL OF APPROVAL

Don't confuse seals with sea lions. If you're picturing an animal clapping its flippers together at a water park as it performs, you've got the wrong animal. Seals belong to a group of animals called pinnipeds, which means "fin-footed." These are divided into true, or earless, seals and eared seals, including sea lions and fur seals. Sea lions walk on land using their large flippers and have ear flaps, whereas true seals have ear holes and four small flippers so they flop around on their bellies. While seals do come on land to mate and give birth, they live mainly in the water. Seals can dive to at least 984 feet deep, with the Southern elephant seal diving to a record 7,835 feet.

Fun Fact
Oddly enough the seal's closest relatives are bears, weasels, raccoons, & skunks.

Did you know...
A seal pup is born with white fur, which it sheds over three to four weeks.

Seals have been known to slap their stomachs with their flippers to warn other seals of predators.

16

Seals have excellent hearing both in and out of the water; their vision is better under water than on land.

HARP SEAL

FACT FILE

CLASS
MAMMAL

GROUP NAME
COLONY, ROOKERY, OR HAREM

TERRITORY
NORTH ATLANTIC AND ARCTIC OCEANS

HOW BIG!

AVERAGE LIFE SPAN
30 YEARS

DIET
CARNIVORE
FISH AND CRUSTACEANS

Did you know...

? Seals can swim up to speeds of 23 mph and may migrate up to 3,100 miles to feed.

HUNTED

Seals keep warm thanks to their soft fur and a thick layer of blubber underneath their skin. Unfortunately, this is also the reason they have been hunted over the years.

How to draw... a seal

1. BODY SHAPE: Draw a vertical oval, and then another diagonal one slightly lower, so they overlap like this.

2. CLEAN UP: We just need the outside shape, so any lines that cut across the shape can be erased.

Erase the inside lines

3. BACK FLIPPERS: Draw some back flippers that are shaped like a fish tail.

4. SIDE FLIPPERS: First, draw an oval on the body for a tummy. Add a little flipper On either side of the body, then erase the original outside body lines.

Erase the original lines

FOR THE MOUTH & NOSE:

1. Draw a kidney bean shape.

2. Add a triangle at the top.

3. Draw two lines down for the mouth..

4. Add three whiskers to each side.

5. CUTE FACE: Draw two lovely round, black eyes. Then follow the steps above to create the mouth and nose area.

6. PLAYFUL PUPS! Your seal pup is playing between the seaweed and rocks. Why don't you add a friend for your seal?

18

SWORDFISH

THIS SPEEDY PREDATOR WOULD WIN IN A DUEL

Can you imagine having a sword for a nose? Well, the swordfish doesn't have to imagine. This predatory fish is famed for its long, sword-like bill, which it uses to defend itself and kill its prey. But the sword isn't its only weapon. One of the ocean's fastest fish, they're built for speed, reaching up to 60 miles per hour. This large and powerful fish averages around 9.8 feet in length, although the females tend to be larger and the longest recorded swordfish measured an impressive 14.9 feet. It might be due to their size and speed, but they don't have many natural predators other than the killer whale or shortfin mako shark.

These strong and aggressive fighters have been known to pierce through the hull of a boat.

Fun Fact
Sword fish leaping from the water may be trying to remove parasites from their bodies.

©Ana Maria Perez Leal/EyeEm/Getty

? Did you know...
Special organs next to their eyes heat their eyes and brain, helping them to see better.

©wildestanimal/Getty

SWORDFISH
FACT FILE

CLASS
FISH

GROUP NAME
FLOTILLA

TERRITORY
WORLDWIDE INCLUDING ATLANTIC, INDIAN, AND PACIFIC OCEANS

AVERAGE LIFE SPAN
NINE YEARS

DIET
CARNIVORE
BONY FISH, SQUID, AND OCTOPUS

HOW BIG!

Did you know...
It's a myth that swordfish stab their prey with their bills; they slash at their food to kill and eat it.

As they grow into adults, swordfish lose their teeth and scales.

GROWING UP FAST
Female swordfish can lay up to 30,000,000 eggs in the water, which the males then fertilize by swimming over them. The larvae, which soon have visible bills, grow quickly. In fact, a swordfish may grow to one million times its size during its lifetime.

21

How to draw... a swordfish

1. EYE-SHAPED BODY: Draw a long eye shape like this.

2. MOUTH AND NOSE: Draw a little mouth and just above this draw a long nose that looks like a sword.

1. Create a little mouth

Erase the original lines afterwards

2. Add the sword nose

3. EYE: First, draw a curved line to separate the head and body. Draw a big eye just in front of this line, like below.

4. FINS: First, draw the big wavy fin all the way along its back. Start higher nearer the head and slope down to the body as you draw. Then directly below, draw a thinner one pointing downwards.

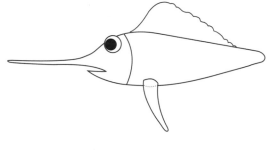

5. FINAL FINS: Draw a tail shape at the end of the body, then add the final fin between this and the bottom fin you drew in step 4.

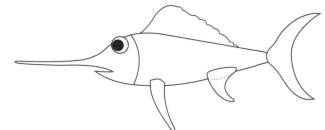

6. SHINY SCALES: We have used different blues to create our finished swordfish. Don't forget to add the lines on the fins and tail.

SEA OTTER

THESE OTTER-LY ADORABLE MAMMALS STICK TOGETHER

Sea otters are one of the cutest critters thanks to their furry coats. In fact, they actually have the densest fur of any animal, with one million hairs per square inch. One of the smallest marine mammals, they're the only ones that don't have blubber to keep them warm. Instead, they have to rub air into their fur to create an insulating, waterproof coat. They may look like they're clapping their hands and feet as they float in the water, but they're actually just keeping their extremities out of the water to retain heat. When they do decide to dive under, they can reach a depth of up to 90 meters (300 feet). This keystone species is vital to its ecosystem, but sadly its numbers are decreasing.

Fun Fact
Their tough teeth can crush clams and even bite through the spines of a sea urchin—ouch!

Did you know...
These hungry mammals eat more than a quarter of their weight in food a day to keep warm.

Wondering where they keep their tools? They have pockets of skin under their arms to store rocks in.

Sea otters feel out their prey using their long whiskers and front paws, as well as their sense of smell.

SEA OTTER
FACT FILE

CLASS
MAMMAL

GROUP NAME
ROMP OR RAFT

TERRITORY
ALONG THE COASTS OF THE PACIFIC OCEAN IN NORTH AMERICA AND ASIA

HOW BIG!

AVERAGE LIFE SPAN
15—20 YEARS

DIET
CARNIVORE
INVERTEBRATES INCLUDING SEA URCHINS, MUSSELS, CLAMS, AND CRABS

CONSERVATION STATUS
ENDANGERED

Did you know...
They are the only marine mammals to use stone tools; this is done to crack open shells.

A LOVE LIKE NO OTTER
Sea otters sleep floating on their backs and can often be seen holding paws with their mates or their pups to stop them from drifting apart. These marine mammals make devoted, attentive mothers and raise their pups alone.

How to draw... an otter

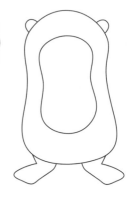

1. BODY: Start by drawing a peanut-shaped body. Then draw a smaller version inside it.

2. EARS AND FEET: At the top add two little ears, and at the bottom two webbed feet.

3. FACE AND TAIL: Add two eyes just above the inside shape, then draw a triangle nose on the line, and a mouth underneath.. Draw a big tail above the right foot.

4. ARMS: Where the body is narrower, add a short arm to each side.

Erase the body lines that go through the arms

5. WHISKERS AND CLAWS: Draw some cute little whiskers. Next, add small claws to the arms, and webbed toes to the feet.

6. COLOR: Give your otter a lovely brown coat to keep it warm in the ice-cold ocean!

SHRIMP

THE TINY CRUSTACEAN MAY BE SHELLFISH, BUT IT THINKS WITH ITS HEART

While shrimp may look similar to prawns, they are different in a few ways, such as being generally smaller and only having claws on two of their five pairs of legs instead of three. Amazingly, there are more than 2,000 different types of shrimp, some you can barely see while others measure up to 12 inches. Their hearts are located in their head to help protect them, but that does mean they don't have very big brains. They do have excellent vision, and the pistol shrimp boasts the fastest eyes of any aquatic animal. Shrimp don't have a backbone either. Instead, they have a hard shell-like exoskeleton, which they shed throughout their lives.

? Did you know...
They form important friendships: the cleaner shrimp cleans parasites off moray eels.

The tiger pistol shrimp produces the loudest sound in the ocean—210 decibels and louder than a gunshot!

Fun Fact

Some species of shrimp glow in the dark thanks to a special kind of bioluminescent bacteria.

TIGER PISTOL SHRIMP

FACT FILE

CLASS
INVERTEBRATE

GROUP NAME
TROUPE

TERRITORY
INDO-WEST PACIFIC OCEAN

HOW SMALL!

AVERAGE LIFE SPAN
3—4 YEARS

DIET
CARNIVORE
SMALLER SHRIMP SPECIES

Some species, like the tiger pistol shrimp, fire bubbles at their enemies by punching their claw forward at 60mph.

? Did you know...

They may be small, but shrimp can be powerful. The Harlequin shrimp use their claws to cut off the arms of starfish to eat.

BREEDING MACHINES

All shrimp are born male and will become female in order to mate. The shellfish breed unbelievably quickly. In fact, they will have already started laying eggs— between 50,000 and one million — by the time their first batch hatches.

How to draw... a shrimp

1. EGG HEAD: Start by drawing an oval-shaped head.

2. SHELL: Behind the head, draw the first section of the armored shell. Behind that, draw the second smaller piece.

1. First section

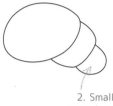

2. Smaller second section

3. TAIL: Draw the third section at the end, and then add a triangle-shaped tail.

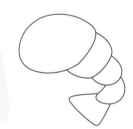

4. FACE: Draw a big eye and a mouth on the head. Then add some lines to the tail.

5. FEELERS AND LEGS: Draw two big, curly feelers coming out from above the mouth. Then add four little feet to the body section under the head.

Clean up any lines that overlap with your eraser

6. COLOR! Shrimp come in a variety of colors and patterns, so you really can choose any color scheme.

STINGRAY

THE PANCAKE FISH WITH A STING IN ITS TAIL

Affectionately known as the "pancake of the sea," this flat-bodied fish is most famous for its stinger, although they're not usually aggressive. The venomous spine in its tail serves as a defense against predators and, although painful, it is not usually fatal to humans unless it strikes the chest or abdomen (as in the case of zoologist Steve Irwin). Closely related to the shark, they too can detect electricity to find their prey, as this can be difficult when your eyes sit on top of your head and your food is swimming below you. They have special organs on the side of their face, which help them sense their food using electric signals in the water.

They have no bones; instead, their exoskeleton is made out of cartilage—the same substance as our ears and nose.

Fun Fact
Greek dentists once used stingray venom as an anaesthetic to help ease tooth pain.

Did you know...
They have openings near their eyes to help them breathe when buried in the sand.

BLUE-SPOTTED STINGRAY

FACT FILE

- - - - - - -

CLASS
FISH

GROUP NAME
FEVER

TERRITORY
INDO-WEST PACIFIC REGION

AVERAGE LIFE SPAN
UNKNOWN

DIET
CARNIVORE
MOLLUSCS, WORMS, SHRIMPS, CRABS, AND SMALL FISH

HOW BIG!

These fish look like birds in the water; they move their bodies by flapping their sides like wings.

? Did you know...
Thanks to their flat bodies and color, stingrays are able to hide from view completely in the sand.

BORN THIS RAY

Stingrays give birth to around two to six babies a year, often after a six to seven month mating period. Their babies are born fully developed and are able to swim and feed without needing to be cared for by their parents.

How to draw... a stingray

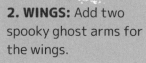

1. CAT HEAD: To start the stingray imagine you are drawing a cat's head and ears.

2. WINGS: Add two spooky ghost arms for the wings.

3. TAIL: Join the wings together at the bottom, and then draw a long lion's tail.

4. FACE: Add two little dots for eyes and a mouth. Draw two small fins at the base of the tail.

5. UNDERSIDE: Following the line at the top of the body, add a line to show the underneath of the wings. Draw a patch of different-sized circles on the body for its skin.

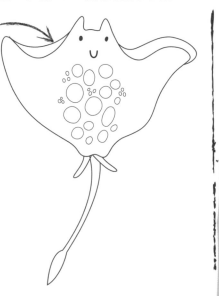

6. TURN YOUR PAPER: Add color and rotate your drawing so it's on its side and your stingray is now ready to glide through the ocean!

PUFFERFISH

THE SPIKY FISH THAT'S READY TO DEFEND ITSELF

If there's one fish you don't want to mess with, it's the pufferfish. Also known as the balloonfish, blowfish, globefish, swellfish, or toadfish, there are around 200 species and they are the most poisonous fish in the sea. Their bodies contain tetrodotoxin, which is 1,200 times more deadly than cyanide. The amount in a pufferfish can kill 30 humans and there is no cure. What's even more surprising is that some humans are brave enough to eat it. The Japanese delicacy (or meal) is known as "fuju," and more than 100 people a year die from eating it. Pufferfish are masters of self-defense—when attacked they can inflate or "puff" themselves up to three to four times their size to scare off predators.

Fun Fact

It seems dolphins get lightheaded and act dopey when they eat pufferfish, according to a BBC One documentary.

©Lotus41/Getty

Did you know...

? Unlike most fish that have scales, pufferfish have poisonous spikes, which act as a means of protection.

They have four teeth, which look like one giant tooth, that never stop growing.

They don't have eyelids; instead they blink by pulling their eyeballs into their sockets.

LONG-SPINED PORCUPINEFISH
FACT FILE

- - - - - - - -

CLASS
FISH

GROUP NAME
SCHOOL

TERRITORY
TROPICAL AND SUBTROPICAL WATERS

AVERAGE LIFE SPAN
UP TO 15 YEARS

DIET
CARNIVORE
INVERTEBRATES INCLUDING SEA URCHINS

HOW SMALL!

? Did you know...
Male pufferfish attract their mates by constructing large geometric patterns in the sand.

CODE RED
Their ballooning skills are not their only defense against predators. Pufferfish can hide by changing color to blend in with their environment if they're in danger. They're slow swimmers, so they need every defense they can get!

How to draw... a pufferfish

1. ROUND BODY:
Draw a big circle.
Nice and easy !

2. BIG CHEEKS: Add two smaller circles halfway up and on a slight angle like this.

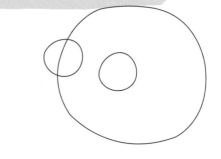

Before you draw the lips, erase the cheek line that goes through the body

3. LIPS: In between the cheeks, draw a fat 8 shape for the lips. Then draw a wavy line through the middle of the lips, under the cheek, to the back of the body.

lips

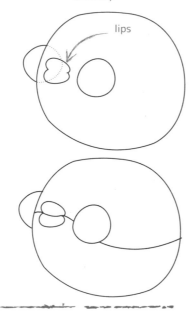

4. GOOGLY EYES: Draw two more circles above the cheeks and lips like this. Then add a wavy tail and side fin..

Erase the line that goes through the eye

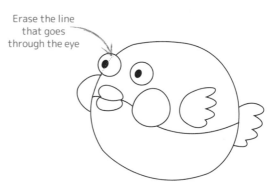

5. SPIKY: Cover your pufferfish in lots of triangle-shaped spikes! Then add lines to the fin and tail.

6. COLOR CHANGING! Pufferfish are known to change color to defend themselves. What color will you choose for your own pufferfish?

NARWHAL

THE ELUSIVE UNICORNS OF THE SEA ARE REAL

Think unicorns aren't real? Think again! These one-horned wonders are toothed whales, but their tooth is a ten-foot spiralling tusk, which protrudes from their head. Known as the "unicorns of the sea" for this reason, scientists aren't actually sure what the purpose of the tusk is. It's thought that it's an important sensory organ, as it has ten million nerve endings and this helps the narwhal sense out food, mates, and even changes to their environment. They have a thick layer of blubber, which makes up 40% of their mass and helps them withstand Arctic temperatures. Most spend up to five months a year under the ice in the Baffin Bay-Davis Strait area between Canada and Greenland.

Fun Fact

Not all narwhals have their trademark tusk; only 15% of females have one.

A narwhal's skin is full of Vitamin C, which is why they are hunted by Inuit people.

©wildestanimal/Getty

Did you know...
Narwhals dive to depths of 4,500 ft in the ocean when fishing.

NARWHAL

FACT FILE

CLASS
MAMMAL

GROUP NAME
BLESSING

TERRITORY
ARCTIC WATERS OF CANADA, GREENLAND, NORWAY, AND RUSSIA

HOW BIG!

AVERAGE LIFE SPAN
25—50 YEARS

DIET
CARNIVORE
HALIBUT, COD, SQUID, AND SHRIMP

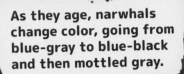

As they age, narwhals change color, going from blue-gray to blue-black and then mottled gray.

Did you know...

These social animals travel in groups of 15—20 whales or super pods of about 100.

ICY THREAT

Narwhals can hold their breath for up to 25 minutes under water. They surface to breathe between cracks in the ice. Their biggest threat is climate change, as they rely on the ice to hide from predators, such as polar bears.

How to draw... a narwhal

1. BODY SHAPE:
Think upside down teardrop or pear—this is the shape we need to start our narwhal drawing.

2. AVOCADO TUMMY:
Draw a smaller version of the shape inside.

3. ADD A TAIL:
Erase the bottom tip of the body and draw a tail on the end.

4. FACE AND TUSK: It's time to draw the famous tusk! Draw a thin cone shape at the top of the head. Add a curved stripe around it. Draw the eyes and mouth underneath.

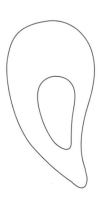

Erase the line that goes through the tusk

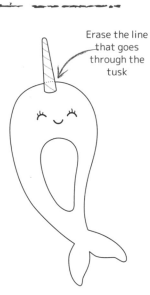

5. FLIPPERS: Draw a flipper on each side. The left one in front of the body and the right behind.

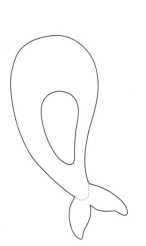

Erase the line that goes through the left flipper

6. COLOR! We used a dark blue for our finished narwhal, and a gray for its tummy and tusk.

CORAL

THE LIVING RAINFORESTS OF THE SEA

Sometimes called "rainforests of the sea," it may surprise you to know that corals are not actually plants, but animals. The branch-like structure that we call coral is actually a colony of thousands of tiny invertebrates called polyps. Hard corals, such as brain corals, use calcium carbonate to produce a hard exoskeleton to build the rock-like reef. Soft corals, such as sea fans, look more like plants and grasses. There are around 6,000 species of coral and they are found all over the world, but the largest reef system is the Great Barrier Reef in Australia. Corals are the world's largest biological structures. They provide food for millions of people, so watch where you tread next time you're on vacation!

As well as food and shelter, corals provide protection from storms to millions of species by acting as a barrier.

Fun Fact

Coral as we know it today has been around for more than 240 million years!

Did you know...

Corals bleach in warm waters and they get their color from an algae called Zooxanthellae.

Even though they only make up 0.1% of the ocean, corals provide a home for more than 25% of all its creatures.

STAGHORN CORAL

FACT FILE

CLASS
INVERTEBRATE

GROUP NAME
COLONY

TERRITORY
THE BAHAMAS, FLORIDA, THE CARIBBEAN, AND AUSTRALIA

AVERAGE LIFE SPAN
HUNDREDS OF YEARS

DIET
OMNIVORE
ALGAE AND PLANKTON

CONSERVATION STATUS
CRITICALLY ENDANGERED

HOW BIG!

Did you know...

Corals need sunlight to grow, but too much heat can be dangerous and even kill them.

CLEAN FREAKS

Corals cannot survive in murky and polluted waters, as they need sunlight to thrive. However, many species of coral filter the water by consuming plankton and organic matter, which improves its quality and clarity.

1. STEM: Draw a "u" shape at the bottom for the stem.

2. ANTLER HORNS: Draw the first small branch on the left. Then, just like an antler, create a three-pronged branch like this.

3. HIGHEST BRANCH: In line with the center of your stem, draw a tall, curvy branch.

4. LAST ONE: To finish, draw the final branch on the right and then join it to the stem at the bottom.

5. COLOR AND SHADE: Choose a color you want the coral to be and color all of it in. Then, on the right side of each of the branches, color with a darker shade so the coral looks 3D.

6. TEXTURE: On top of the shading, add dots of a different color for the rough texture of the coral.

SPERM WHALE

YOU COULD CALL THIS BRAINY MAMMAL VERY BIG-HEADED

When it comes to heads, it doesn't get bigger than this. The sperm whale not only has the biggest animal head, but the largest brain too. With an average weight of 17 pounds, that's five times heavier than a human brain. The largest of the toothed whales, males can grow up to 68 feet and weigh up to 45 tons. The toothed whales have a poor sense of taste and smell, so they rely heavily on sound. Luckily for them, they're also the planet's loudest animal, with clicks of 230 decibels—that's louder than a one-ton bomb. They use their clicks to locate their prey by echolocation and to recognize other sperm whales.

Fun Fact
Sperm whales feed constantly consuming 3% of their body weight in a day.

©wildestanimal/Getty

Did you know...
Females and young males socialize in pods of 15—20; males are solitary except for breeding.

Its blowhole is unique, set at an angle on the left side of its head. It can spray water up to 16.4 ft high.

FACT FILE

- - - - - - -

CLASS
MAMMAL

GROUP NAME
POD

TERRITORY
**DEEP OCEANS
WORLDWIDE FROM
THE EQUATOR
TO THE ARCTIC AND
ANTARCTIC**

AVERAGE LIFE SPAN
UP TO 70 YEARS

DIET
CARNIVORE
SQUID, OCTOPUS,
AND FISH

HOW
BIG!

Their conical-shaped teeth measure 3.94—7.88 in long and weigh up to 2.2 lbs.

Did you know...

They have been recorded reaching a depth of 9,816 ft and they can hold their breath for 90 minutes.

VERTICAL SLEEP

Sperm whales are the least sleep dependent mammals on Earth, napping for only 10 to 15 minutes at a time. And when they do sleep, they do so in a vertical position while not breathing and remaining completely motionless.

©Westend61/Getty

©Gerard Soury/Getty

How to draw... a sperm whale

1. LONG BODY: Start drawing a rectangular shape with a rounded corner like this.

2. JAW: Underneath this, draw another line for the jaw.

3. START OF THE TAIL: From both ends of the body, draw upwards so the lines come together.

4. FLIPPY TAIL: Draw two leaf shapes at the end for the tail fins. At the bottom of the body, add a little fin.

After drawing the fin, erase this line.

5. SMILE: Draw a big smile and a "u" shaped eye. Add some lines to the fin and tail.

6. BLUE HUE: Choose your favorite blue to turn your whale into a majestic creature of the ocean.

GIANT SQUID

THIS MYSTERIOUS SEA MONSTER HAS NO TROUBLE SEEING IN THE DARKEST DEPTHS

The world's largest invertebrate, the giant squid, is believed to be the inspiration behind the myths and legends of giant sea monsters. It has been known to grow up to 59 feet and have the longest tentacles of any cephalopod (that's the octopus, squid, and cuttlefish family). Not only that, but its eyes, which are 10 inches in diameter, are the largest in the animal kingdom. This means it has no trouble seeing in the dark depths of the ocean and it can catch its prey from up to 33 feet away. This elusive squid has escaped scientists ever since they knew it existed, and wasn't even caught live on camera until 2004.

Once it catches its prey, the giant squid uses the radula, a tooth-covered tongue inside its beak, to eat.

These masters of camouflage are able to change color and regenerate their arms.

Did you know... The giant squid's arms are covered in sucker cups with serrated circles to grip prey.

© RubenEarth/Getty

GIANT SQUID
FACT FILE

CLASS
INVERTEBRATE

GROUP NAME
SHOAL

TERRITORY
OCEANS WORLDWIDE

HOW BIG!

AVERAGE LIFE SPAN
5 YEARS

DIET
CARNIVORE
FISH, SHRIMP AND OTHER SQUID

Fun Fact
Footage from a remotely operated camera has shown giant squid eating each other.

Did you know...
? It's thought up to 131 million giant squid are consumed by sperm whales every year.

A GIANT ENIGMA
Everything we know about the giant squid we know because of specimens washed up on our beaches. That's why researchers aren't really sure if the giant squid is just one species. Some think there are as many as eight different species.

How to draw...   a giant squid

1. TEARDROP: Draw a long teardrop shape like this.

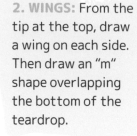

2. WINGS: From the tip at the top, draw a wing on each side. Then draw an "m" shape overlapping the bottom of the teardrop.

3. TENTACLES: Draw the first of the tentacles from the "m" shape. For the second one, loop it up around the first and add an oval to the end.

Erase the bottom teardrop line

4. MORE TENTACLES: Draw another two shorter ones in the middle. Then add another looped tentacle before adding the final one that will join to the other end of the "m" shape.

5. FACE AND STRIPES: Add the face above the tentacles and some stripes to the body and wings.

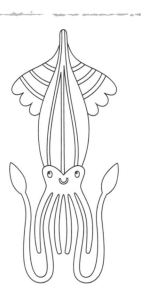

6. STRIPY! As you color in the limbs, why not add some more stripes in two different colors?

LEATHERBACK TURTLE

THIS GIANT REPTILE IS A TURTLE-Y AWESOME RECORD-BREAKER

The leatherback turtle is not only the fourth largest reptile on Earth, but also the world's largest turtle. It can measure up to 6.6 feet long and weigh up to 1,984 pounds. These powerful swimmers are also the deepest diving turtles. They can drop up to 3,940 feet thanks to a thick layer of insulating fat, and can hold their breath for up to 85 minutes. To top it off, they also have the widest distribution of all marine turtles. Leatherbacks migrate huge distances, traveling up to 10,000 miles a year. These amazing giants have been around for more than 100 million years and, although they're big travelers, they're not going anywhere.

It gets its name because its shell isn't hard like other sea turtles, but kind of leathery.

© Herve06/Getty

? Did you know...

Just one in every 1,000 leatherback turtles survives to adulthood.

They are powered by strong front flippers that measure up to 8.9 ft.

LEATHERBACK TURTLE

FACT FILE

- - - - - - -

CLASS
REPTILE

GROUP NAME
BALE, NEST, OR DOLE

TERRITORY
ATLANTIC, PACIFIC, AND INDIAN OCEANS

AVERAGE LIFE SPAN
UP TO 50 YEARS

DIET
CARNIVORE
INVERTEBRATES SUCH AS JELLYFISH

HOW BIG!

Fun Fact
Leather back turtles can eat up to 73% of their own body weight in jellyfish each day.

Did you know...
Unlike other sea turtles, leatherback turtles often change nesting sites.

THE LOST YEARS
Leatherback turtles nest every two to three years, laying up to around 100 eggs. Babies return to the sea once they hatch, but scientists have called the period between hatching and adulthood as the "lost years," as juveniles have proven hard to study in the ocean.

How to draw... a turtle

1. PEBBLE SHAPE:
Draw a smooth pebble shape, with a slightly pointed end on the left.

2. HEAD:
Next, create a smaller circle for the head. Draw it away from the body like this.

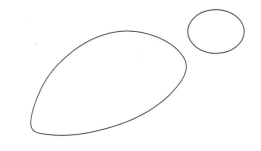

3. NECK AND MOUTH:
Join the head to the body with a neck. Then erase the line at the bottom of the head to make the head and neck one shape. Draw a mouth and shape the nose.

1. Add the neck

2. Erase the line here

3. Add a mouth

4. FLIPPERS:
Draw a front and back flipper, then add a crescent moon-shaped eye.

5. SHELL PATTERN:
First add a few spots on the flippers and head. Then it's time to design your shell pattern! What will you choose? Shapes, swirls or twirls?

6. COLOR:
We have used lots of different greens for our sea turtle, but you can choose whatever colors you want. It would look great with a rainbow-colored shell!

59

STARFISH

THIS BEAUTIFUL INVERTEBRATE ISN'T THAT BRIGHT

Despite their name, starfish are not actually fish and many aren't even star-shaped! Also called sea stars, they're most closely related to sea urchins and sea cucumbers. There are more than 2,000 species of this beautiful invertebrate and they come in all shapes, sizes, and colors. Most weigh around 10.8 pounds and have five arms. However, the largest of these—the sunflower sea star—has up to 24 arms and can weigh up to 13.4 pounds. Starfish don't swim and have no fins or gills. They have no brain, no blood, and no bones either. They cannot survive in fresh water as their bodies rely on salt to survive. Instead, they filter sea water through their bodies for nutrients.

Fun Fact
The sun star, leather star & crown-of-thorns starfish have venomous spines.

Did you know...
They are able to eat prey much bigger than them because they have two stomachs.

Instead of eyes, starfish have eyespots at the tip of each arm, which they use to sense light.

Starfish are hard to kill because they can grow back their own arms; they only need a segment with one cell to regenerate.

SUNFLOWER SEA STAR,

FACT FILE

CLASS
INVERTEBRATE

GROUP NAME
GALAXY OR CONSTELLATION

TERRITORY
EASTERN PACIFIC OCEAN

AVERAGE LIFE SPAN
20.5—65 YEARS

DIET
CARNIVORE
SEA URCHINS, FISH, MOLLUSCS, AND CRUSTACEANS

CONSERVATION STATUS
CRITICALLY ENDANGERED

HOW BIG!

Did you know...

They have hundreds of tube feet under their arms, which they use to move slowly across the sea floor.

A STAR IS BORN

Sea stars can reproduce sexually (by mating with another starfish) or asexually (by themselves by regenerating). Female starfish are able to produce millions of eggs at once, but only a small number survive to adulthood.

How to draw... a starfish

1. FIRST ARM:
Start by drawing around an egg cup, or something small and round. Draw lightly, as this won't be in the final drawing. At the very top, add a triangle shape.

First of the starfish's arms

Lightly draw a circle for a guide

2. ARMS:
Draw another two arms on the right side of the circle.

3. FIVE ARMS:
On the lefthand side, create two more arms that look the same as the other side, until they join up at the top and bottom.

4. FACE:
Erase the circle guide in the middle. Now draw cute eyes and a mouth in the middle of your starfish.

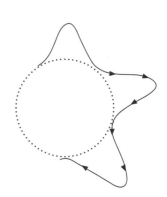

5. TEXTURE AND PATTERN:
Decorate the arms of your starfish with a circle pattern like this, or use dots, lines, or zig zags!

6. SHADING:
To make the arms feel 3D, use a slightly darker shade in between each one like this.

PENGUIN

THESE TUXEDO-WEARING BIRDS ARE IN DISGUISE

The classic black-and-white feathers and comedic waddle are the perfect camouflage. When seen from below, their white bellies blend in with the light colors near the surface of the water. From above, they look a similar color to the darker ocean colors below to hide from predators. Most scientists believe there are 17 species of penguin and all of these live in the southern hemisphere. These waterproof birds cannot fly, but when they jump out of the water, they can leap around 9.8 feet in the air. They are also super swimmers. The Gentoo penguin can swim up to 22 miles per hour, and the Emperor penguin can dive to depths of 1,500 feet.

Penguins are able to drink salt water as they sneeze out the salt thanks to a special gland in their beak.

Fun Fact
Penguins have very fast metabolisms & can poop every 20 minutes.

? Did you know...
Their giant colonies, called rookeries, can include up to a million nesting pairs.

Most birds have circular pupils, but during daylight hours, the king penguin has square pupils.

KING PENGUIN

FACT FILE

- - - - - - - -

CLASS
BIRD

GROUP NAME
WADDLE OR RAFT

TERRITORY
MOST OF THE SUB-ANTARCTIC ISLANDS

HOW BIG!

AVERAGE LIFE SPAN
26 YEARS

DIET
CARNIVORE
LANTERNFISH AND SQUID

Did you know...
Unlike other birds, penguins shed their feathers all at once. This is often called a catastrophic molt.

P-P-P-PUCKER UP!

Most penguin species mate for life. They have some interesting mating habits, from presenting their loved one with a pebble to waving their flippers. Apart from the emperor and king penguins, other species lay two eggs. They take it in turns to keep them warm.

How to draw... a penguin

1. BODY: Start by drawing a shape that looks like a fingernail, with a big arch at the top, and a flatter curve for the bottom.

2. HEAD: Following the line of the body, draw a tall "m" with long legs inside the original shape.

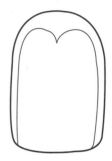

3. EYES AND BEAK: Underneath the "m" add two little eyes like this. Then draw an upside down triangle for its beak.

3. WINGS: Halfway down the body, draw a wing on the left and right sides.

5. FLIPPERS: Draw two cute little feet at the base of the body.

Erase the lines where the wings meet the body

6. BLACK AND WHITE?! OR A COLORFUL PENGUIN? It's completely up to you! We've added some lines to its tummy for feathers.

CLOWNFISH

THESE FISH KEEP THEIR FRIENDS CLOSE AND THEIR ANEMONES CLOSER

If you've seen Disney's *Finding Nemo*, you'll instantly recognize the common clownfish with its bright orange color and white stripes. However, there are 28 different species of clownfish that come in a variety of colors. Also called anemonefish, this reef dweller makes its home in sea anemones in warm, shallow waters off the coast of Australia and Southeast Asia. Closely related to jellyfish and corals, sea anemones deliver poisonous stings to shock their prey, but clownfish are immune to these toxins. Sea anemones share a special bond with the tropical fish: the clownfish removes parasites from the anemone and, in turn, the anemone provides it with shelter.

This tiny fish has some predators including stingrays, sharks, and eels, but its biggest threat is the human pet trade.

? Did you know...

Look inside the clownfish's mouth and you might spot a tongue-eating louse, a parasite that's replaced the fish's tongue.

As odd as it sounds, these fish aren't great swimmers and may get their name from their waddle-like movements.

COMMON CLOWNFISH

FACT FILE

Fun Fact
They often lay their eggs under a full moon and dad babysits until they've hatched.

CLASS
FISH

GROUP NAME
SCHOOL

TERRITORY
SOUTHWEST PACIFIC OCEAN, INDIAN OCEAN, AND RED SEA

HOW SMALL!

AVERAGE LIFE SPAN
6—10 YEARS

DIET
OMNIVORE
ALGAE, ZOOPLANKTON, WORMS, AND SMALL CRUSTACEANS

? Did you know...
Female clownfish lay around 100 to 1,000 eggs. The male then swims over the eggs to fertilize them.

BOYS BECOME GIRLS

Clownfish are hermaphrodites, which means that they change from a female to a male fish at one point in their life. They live in groups and when the dominant female of the group dies, her male partner changes gender to take on her role.

© Westend61/Getty

69

How to draw... a clown fish

1. Draw this shape for the body.

1. BODY AND TAIL: Draw an eye shape, with a slightly fat end on the left. Then on the right, add a tail shape like this.

2. Add the tail fin

2. FINS: Add two more fins on both the top and bottom of the fish's body.

Erase the original body line here

3. EYE AND MOUTH: Give your fish a little smile and an eye.

4. FIN EDGING: On each of the fins and the tail draw on some black curvy tips like below.

5. STRIPES: Add three curved stripes to the body—one by the tail, one in the middle, and one next to the face.

6. NEMO ORANGE! Clownfish are known for their bright orange and white coloring. Why not use a darker orange for the fins and add some scales to its body?

HAMMERHEAD SHARK

THE FISH WITH A METAL DETECTOR FOR A HEAD

The hammerhead is one of the most recognizable sharks with its "T"-shaped head, but this odd trait comes in handy. Its eyes sit on the outer edge of the mallet shape, which means it has 360-degree vision and can see above and below itself at the same time. Of course, this doesn't mean it'll always see you coming—it has a blind spot right in front of its nose. However, hammerheads have a far more powerful sense than sight: their heads, which act like metal detectors, scanning the seafloor for prey hiding in the sand. They have a special organ called the Ampullae of Lorenzini, which contains electrical receptors that pick up electrical pulses emitted by other species.

Out of the nine species, the largest is the great hammerhead, measuring up to 20 ft.

Did you know...

Their favorite food is the stingray; they even seem immune to the venomous spine.

They use their wide heads to pin down prey before eating.

GREAT HAMMERHEAD SHARK

FACT FILE

- - - - - - -

CLASS
FISH

GROUP NAME
GAM, HERD, FRENZY, SCHOOL, OR SHIVER

TERRITORY
TROPICAL WATERS WORLDWIDE

HOW BIG!

AVERAGE LIFE SPAN
20—30 YEARS

DIET
CARNIVORE
FISH, CEPHALOPODS, AND CRUSTACEANS

CONSERVATION STATUS
CRITICALLY ENDANGERED

Fun Fact
Hammerhead sharks are one of the few animals that can get a tan.

Did you know...
? Hammerheads live in large schools of up to 500 fish, but at night they hunt alone.

SIDEWAYS SWIM

Hammerheads can often be found swimming sideways! It seems this is more efficient, as their dorsal fin is longer than their pectoral fin, making swimming straight more effort. These fish can swim up to 25 mph and migrate distances of up to 765 miles.

How to draw... a hammerhead shark

1. THE HEAD: Start by copying this shape to create our shark's head!

2. TUMMY AND TAIL: Now add the shark's body and tail underneath.

3. JOINING THE SHAPES: Erase all the inside lines so you make one complete shape. Then carefully draw a curved line from the head to the tail, like below.

Erase the original lines

New line to draw

4. FINS: Draw a dorsal fin on its back, and then add two side fins to its body.

5. FACE: Draw a small circle on each side of the head, then add a big smile underneath. Lastly, draw three curved lines on its side for the gills.

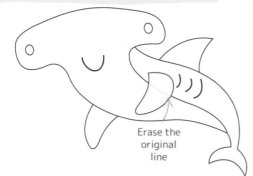

Erase the original line

6. TWO-TONE GRAY: Use a light gray for the tummy and face, and then a darker gray for the side, tail, and fins.

CRAB

THE CRUSTACEAN THAT TAKES A SIDEWAYS APPROACH

Crabs are decapods, meaning they have ten legs, which they famously use for walking sideways. However, many can also walk forward, backward, and diagonally, it's just not as quick or easy. Two of their legs are pincers or claws, which they use for hunting, crushing the shells of their prey, and fighting. Their bodies are made up of a hard exoskeleton, which they shed as they grow. It varies by species, but female blue crabs can lay as many as eight million eggs at once, which they then keep on their bellies until fertilization. The eggs are then released into the water where they hatch into larvae and then continue to molt until they drop to the sea floor as fully formed juveniles.

© Jeffrey Hamilton/Getty

Fun Fact
Blue crabs are only pregnant for 1—2 weeks. Now that's a short pregnancy!

© Jack Andersen/Getty

? Did you know...
Just like fish, crabs have gills, which they use to breathe, although they can survive out of the water.

Fossils of crabs have been found from over 200 million years ago.

They don't need to worry about losing a limb in a fight, because they will regenerate after about a year.

BLUE CRAB
FACT FILE
- - - - - -

CLASS
INVERTEBRATE

GROUP NAME
CAST

TERRITORY
ATLANTIC COAST AND GULF OF MEXICO

HOW SMALL!

AVERAGE LIFE SPAN
1—3 YEARS

DIET
OMNIVORE
MUSSELS, SNAILS, FISH, PLANTS, AND SMALL CRUSTACEANS

? **Did you know...**
Crabs communicate by rubbing, waving, or drumming their claws, or rubbing the ridges against their legs.

ALL SIZES
There are around 7,000 species of crab worldwide. They range in size from the pea crab, which is only a few millimeters long, to the Japanese spider crab, which has been known to reach an incredible 12.5 ft long.

How to draw... a crab

1. SQUASHED CIRCLE: To start, draw a flattened circle, just like a pebble.

2. EYE, EYE: On top of the body, draw two circles on sticks for the crab's eyes.

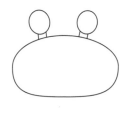

3. SNIP, SNIP: On each side of the body, about halfway down, draw two big half-moon shapes for the claws.

4. LEGS: Just under the left claw, add four little legs. On the righthand side, draw them on top of the body, like this.

5. LOTS OF LASHES: Draw some long lashes onto the eye stalks, and a big smile on the middle of the body.

6. SHADING: To make your crab 3D, use a slightly darker shade at the bottom of the body, claws and legs, to create shadow. Add some rosy cheeks and shell texture to finish off your cute crab!

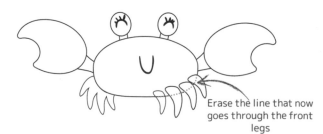

Erase the line that now goes through the front legs

Use a darker shade to add shadows

78

OCTOPUS

EIGHT IS THE MAGIC NUMBER FOR THIS INK-CREDIBLE CEPHALOPOD

Everyone knows that octopuses have eight tentacles, right? Wrong—they actually don't! They have six arms and two legs, which they can regrow. Tentacles are longer and only have suckers at the tips, whereas a Giant Pacific octopus's arm has 280 suckers, which are used to taste. This invertebrate doesn't have bones either, which enables them to squeeze through small crevices. It does, however, have three hearts and blue blood! Octopuses use ink to escape their predators, but they are also venomous. Although the octopus species has existed for nearly 300 million years, male octopuses have a lifespan ranging from just six months to a few years and sadly die not long after mating.

They do not have ears and rely on their eyesight to avoid predators.

© Stuart Westmorland/Getty

© Andrey Nekrasov/Getty

? Did you know...
Masters of camouflage, octopuses can change color to blend in with their surroundings.

Octopuses do not have teeth; instead they have a sharp parrot-like beak where their arms meet.

GIANT PACIFIC OCTOPUS

FACT FILE

CLASS
INVERTEBRATE

GROUP NAME
COLONY

TERRITORY
PACIFIC OCEAN

AVERAGE LIFE SPAN
3—5 YEARS

DIET
CARNIVORE
SHRIMP, CLAMS, LOBSTERS, AND FISH. KNOWN TO ALSO EAT SHARKS AND BIRDS

HOW BIG!

Fun Fact
These intelligent creatures are the only invertebrates that are able to use tools.

? Did you know...
Neurons in an octopus's arms mean they can react even if separated from the body.

SHELL COLLECTORS

It seems octopuses might enjoy collecting crustacean shells. Researchers have studied their behavior and found that they use the shells for shelter or protection, to build a garden or fort, or even to decorate their homes.

How to draw... an octopus

1. HEAD: Start off by drawing a circle. This will be the head of the octopus.

2. FIRST OF MANY: Let's start on the arms! Draw a curved line up past the top of the head. When it's the right length, draw a curved tip and head back down to the body. Follow the shape of the first line as best you can.

1. Draw up to the tip of the arm

2. Then follow the line back to the body, like this

3. THREE MORE TO GO! Add three more wavy arms. These will be the ones at the front of the body, so erase the bottom of the circle once you have finished.

Erase the original head line

4. FACE: Draw two "n"-shaped eyes, and then a "u" shape underneath for the mouth. Add two small circles for the cute rosy cheeks.

Erase any arm lines that overlap

5. MORE ARMS & LEGS: An octopus needs six arms and two legs! Draw four more dangly arms/legs behind the front ones. They don't have to be in the exact same place as ours.

6. COLOR: Many Octopuses can change color! Some have bumpy skin or patches of color. So make yours super colorful!

MANATEE

EATING IS A NO-BRAINER FOR THIS SEA COW

Think how long you spend eating in an average day. One or two hours? How about 12? That's how long manatees spend eating each day to survive. They can consume up to 10% of their body weight—about 1,200 pounds of plants a day including sea grass, mangrove leaves, and algae. Known as sea cows because of their slow-moving nature and grass-eating ways, these aquatic mammals can swim up to 20 miles per hour, but tend to paddle lazily along at five miles per hour. Their brain-to-body ratio is the lowest of any mammal. Luckily for them, they don't have to be smart or fast, as they have no natural predators to outswim.

Fun Fact
Surprisingly, their closest living relatives are elephants and hyraxes.

Did you know...
Manatees swim to the surface every three to five minutes to breathe, but can hold their breath for 20 minutes.

Manatee teeth grow continually through their lives; the new ones push forward to replace the old ones.

Manatees don't have necks. They're one of only two mammals with six vertebrae and can't turn their heads.

WEST INDIAN
MANATEE,

FACT FILE
- - - - - -

CLASS
MAMMAL

GROUP NAME
AGGREGATION

TERRITORY
ALONG THE COAST OF FLORIDA, THE GULF COAST, AND THE CARIBBEAN

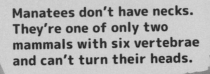

HOW BIG!

AVERAGE LIFE SPAN
30—40 YEARS

DIET
HERBIVORE
AQUATIC PLANTS

? Did you know...

The largest herbivores in the ocean, they grow to 13 ft and weigh on average 1,200 lbs.

MERMAIDS OF THE OCEAN

Oddly enough, sailors once confused manatees with mermaids. This bulbous aquatic mammal looks nothing like a mermaid, but their scientific name, Sirenia, brings to mind the siren mermaids, who lured sailors to their doom.

How to draw... a manatee

1. BODY AND HEAD: For the start of our manatee, we need two ovals that overlap, like this.

2. TAIL: At the bottom of the larger oval, draw a tail.

Erase this line

3. FLIPPERS: Draw two flipper shapes just under its chin.

Erase this line where the tail joins the body

4. FACE: Draw an eye and a big smile underneath.

Erase this line that goes through the front flipper

5. SEAWEED: This manatee looks hungry! Draw a piece of seaweed from the bottom of its mouth.

Erase the chin line that goes through the seaweed

6. WHISKERS: Add some lighter colored spots to the body for that perfect manatee look. Then use a darker color to dab on lots of stubbly whiskers to its nose.

SEAHORSE

HOLD YOUR HORSES! IT'S THE MALE SEAHORSE THAT GIVES BIRTH

Seahorses are surprising in more ways than one. You might not believe they're fish, as they don't have scales, but a hard exoskeleton instead. They're so bony that, apart from the crab, they don't have many predators. Seahorses are one of only a few fish that swim vertically. They do this by flapping their dorsal fin and adjusting their buoyancy using their swim bladder. But the most surprising fact is that female seahorses don't give birth. It's actually the male who carries the babies! Seahorses are monogamous, which means they mate with one partner for life. They get together by performing a mating ritual, which can last up to eight hours. Sadly, only one in 100 babies survive to adulthood.

Seahorses are able to see forwards and backwards at the same time, as their eyes work independently from each other.

©Andrey Nekrasov/Getty

©AndreyNekrasov/Getty

Did you know...
Seahorses have special organs, which allow them to change color and stay camouflaged.

Seahorses use their strong, prehensile tails to hold on to objects and, when they mate, they link tails—like holding hands!

SHORT-SNOUTED SEAHORSE
FACT FILE

CLASS
FISH

GROUP NAME
HERD

TERRITORY
UK, BAY OF BISCAY & MEDITERRANEAN

HOW SMALL!

AVERAGE LIFE SPAN
UP TO 10 YEARS

DIET
CARNIVORE
CRUSTACEANS SUCH AS SHRIMP, CRABS, AND PLANKTON

Fun Fact
Funnily enough, seahorse means "horse caterpillar" in Latin.

Did you know...
Seahorses are slow! The slowest fish in the sea, the dwarf seahorse, swims at 0.01mph.

THE HUNGRY CATERPILLAR
Seahorses have huge appetites. They have such fast digestive systems that they must eat constantly to survive. These fish eat up to 3,000 crustaceans a day, sucking them in through their snouts, which can expand for food.

How to draw... a seahorse

1. EGG HEAD: Draw an egg shape on its side for the head. Then draw two "s"-shaped lines from the bottom of the head, like this.

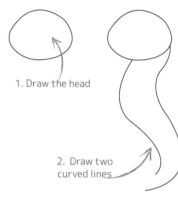

1. Draw the head

2. Draw two curved lines

2. CURLY TAIL: This part is a bit tricky, so it might take a few tries. Draw a curl for the tail. (shown in black). When you get to the end, draw the same shape back (shown in orange) to join the other body line.

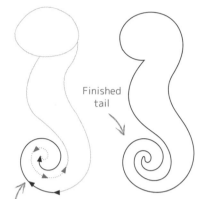

Finished tail

1. From the outside line, draw a twirl. Then follow the line back to the other end of the body

3. SNOUT: On the lefthand side of the head, draw the seahorse's snout.

Erase the line here

4. WINGS AND CREST: Create a little wing on its back, and a wavy crest on top of the head.

5. FACE AND TUMMY: Add a mouth and an eye to the face, and some stripes on its tummy.

6. COLOR! Why not draw some seaweed for your shy little seahorse to hide in?

90

WALRUS

BREAKING THE ICE WITH THIS TUSKY HEAVYWEIGHT

It's no surprise these ocean beasts have been nicknamed the "giants of the Arctic." They can reach lengths of 11.8 feet and weigh over 1.5 tons. Their most distinctive feature, however, is their tusks, which can measure up to 34.5 inches. They're used for fighting, defense, climbing onto ice floats, and as a tool. They can also break through eight inches of ice. There are two species of walrus: the Pacific walrus that lives in Alaska and Russia, and the Atlantic walrus, which can be found in Canada and Greenland. But while they love to rest on the ice, they spend two thirds of their lives in the water, diving up to 295 feet for food.

Walruses have around 400 to 700 sensitive whiskers, which they use as feelers to find their prey.

?Did you know...
These social animals gather in large herds, but males and females tend to hang out in separate groups.

Fun Fact

Its scientific name, *Odobenus rosmarus* means "tooth-walking seahorse" in Latin.

WALRUS FACT FILE

CLASS
MAMMAL

GROUP NAME
HERD

TERRITORY
THE PACIFIC, ATLANTIC AND ARCTIC OCEANS

HOW BIG!

AVERAGE LIFE SPAN
40 YEARS

DIET
CARNIVORE
MOLLUSCS, CLAMS, WORMS, CRUSTACEANS, AND SEA CUCUMBERS

A thick layer of blubber and the ability to slow its heartbeat means the walrus can withstand temperatures of -31°F.

Did you know...

Walruses can sleep under water, as they have pouches under their throats that can hold up to 13 gallons of air.

HAVE A NICE TRIP

A walrus may migrate up to 1,863 miles in search of the best ice. While they tend to move slowly, swimming at around 4 mph, they can reach speeds of 22 mph if needed, and also ride ice floes to get around.

How to draw... a walrus

1. BODY: Start by drawing a potato shape for the body. Then, on the righthand side, add a tail that's shaped a bit like a slug's tail.

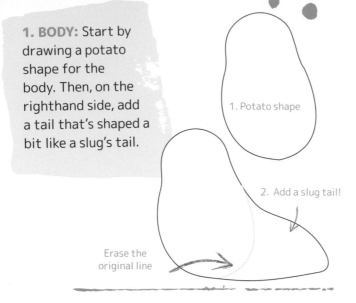

1. Potato shape

2. Add a slug tail!

Erase the original line

2. FACE: Add two eyes, and then a big moustache shape underneath.

3. NOSE AND MOUTH: At the top of the moustache, draw an oval nose and two nostrils. Then add a little loop for the mouth.

4. TUSKS AND WHISKERS: Draw two big tusks down from the mouth and nose. Then add some lovely whiskers!

5. FLIPPERS: Draw two front flippers – one behind its body (1), then one in the middle (2). Finally, add the last flipper at the back (3).

Don't forget to erase the lines that go through the flippers!

1

2

3

6. COLOR! Will your walrus be sitting on a beach? Or on a rock looking out to sea? Add some lines to the flippers, and some fur texture on its back.

ANGLERFISH

THE GHOULISH FISH THAT GLOWS IN THE DARK

Known as one of the ugliest animals on the planet, this angry-looking sea creature generally lives up to a mile below the surface in the darkest depths of the ocean. Female anglerfish catch their prey by using part of their spine as a glow-in-the-dark fishing rod to draw them in. These large predators are usually the size of a football, but can grow up to 3.3 feet long. They have big heads and sharp teeth, which allow them to swallow prey twice their size. They can swim fast when they feel like they are in danger, but tend to drift in the water to save energy, because dinner isn't always on the table when you live at the bottom of the sea.

Not all anglerfish are grayish-brown deep-sea creatures! Some are colorful and live in shallow, tropical waters.

? **Did you know…**
Male anglerfish are parasites, attaching themselves to females using their teeth.

Luckily, this fish isn't fussy—its teeth are bent inward so it can't spit out its food.

DEEP SEA ANGLERFISH

FACT FILE

CLASS
FISH

GROUP NAME
SCHOOL

TERRITORY
WORLDWIDE

AVERAGE LIFE SPAN
**AROUND
24 YEARS**

DIET
CARNIVORE
FISH, CRUSTACEANS,
AND CEPHALOPODS

Fun Fact
A female anglerfish usually carries more than six males on her body to mate with.

HOW
SMALL!

Did you know...

? There are around 200 species of anglerfish, which are made up of frogfish, batfish, goosefish, and the deep-sea angler.

A GLOWING FRIENDSHIP

The glow at the end of the female anglerfish's dorsal spine comes from bioluminescent bacteria. The two share a symbiotic relationship: the bacteria glows to help the anglerfish attract food and, in turn, the bacteria gets protection and nutrients from the anglerfish.

How to draw... an anglerfish

1. EGG SHAPE: Start with a shape that looks like an egg on its side. Then draw in a mouth shape on the lefthand side, like this.

1. Draw an egg on its side

2. Draw a mouth and erase the original line

2. GNASHERS: Inside the mouth add some really sharp teeth. Then add a small eye above.

3. FINS AND TAIL: On the top and bottom of the body, create some wavy fins. Then add a big tail at the back.

4. LURE: Draw an arch (like a rainbow) from the top of the head. The end should be in line with the eye. Then add the all-important light on the end.

5. LITTLE FIN: In the middle of the body, draw a smaller side fin..

6. DEEP, DARK OCEAN: You could create a dark background so the bright yellow lure stands out to attract its prey!

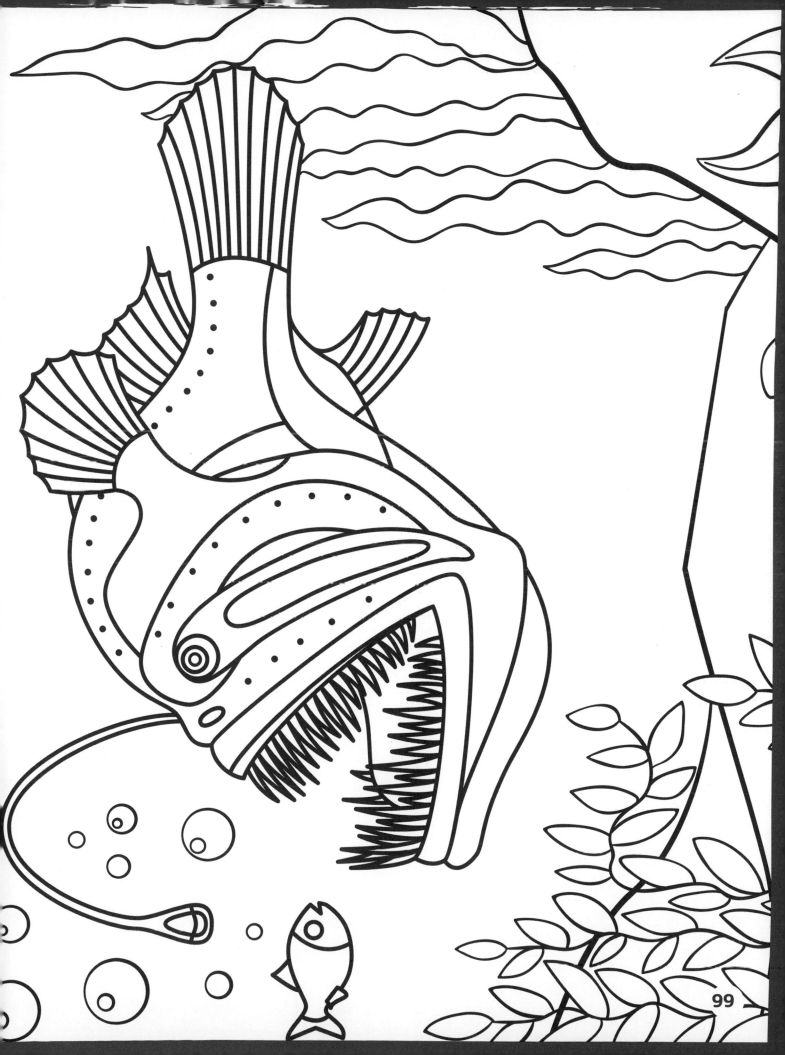

JELLYFISH

THESE SEE-THROUGH STINGERS OUTLIVED DINOSAURS

These translucent creatures may look harmless and be made of 98% water, but watch out: they have a real sting in their tail! The jellyfish's sting can be deadly—the box jellyfish contains enough venom to kill 60 humans—and they can sting you even when they're dead. Despite their name, jellyfish are not actually fish—they're a type of plankton and the oldest multi-organ animal on Earth. In fact, they've existed for more than 600 million years—before dinosaurs. One species, Turritopsis dohrnii, is immortal as it has adapted to age backwards. They may not have a brains, bones, or a heart, but they're pretty tough. Surprisingly, though, most jellyfish live for less than a year.

Did you know...
These beautiful animals can glow in the dark thanks to a phenomenon called bioluminescence.

Its long tentacles measure up to 124 ft, making it the second longest animal.

Jellyfish range in size, but the largest is the lion's mane with a bell diameter of 7 ft 6 in.

LION'S MANE JELLYFISH

FACT FILE

CLASS
INVERTEBRATE

GROUP NAME
SWARM OR BLOOM

TERRITORY
ARCTIC, NORTH PACIFIC, AND NORTH ATLANTIC OCEANS

AVERAGE LIFE SPAN
1 YEAR

DIET
CARNIVORE
PLANKTON, SMALL FISH, CRUSTACEANS, AND OTHER JELLYFISH

HOW BIG!

Fun Fact

It may not sound very pleasant, but jellyfish eat & poop from the same hole.

Did you know...

About 150 million people worldwide are stung by jellyfish a year—hundreds fatally.

JET PROPULSION

Jellyfish don't have legs. Instead, they propel themselves forward through the ocean by contracting their muscles to draw water in and then shooting it out of their mouths. Their mouths are found on the underside of the umbrella-shaped bell.

1. RAINBOW: Draw a rainbow arch with a flat bottom.

2. FRILLY SKIRT: At the bottom of the body shape, draw a frilly skirt, a bit like a tutu. Then erase the original body line underneath.

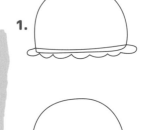

1.

2.

Erase the line that goes through the frill

3. TENTACLES: Underneath the skirt, start drawing wavy tentacles.

4. ADD MORE: Keep adding more until you're happy with how your jellyfish looks.

5. FACE: Give your jellyfish a face. You can also add some thinner, curlier tentacles too. This might be best to do in the color you want them to be, or just leave it as it is.

6. COLOR! Jellyfish can be so many beautiful colors. Have fun choosing what color your jellyfish will be.

BULL SHARK

THE PREDATOR THAT INSPIRED JAWS

The infamous 1975 disaster movie *Jaws* might star a great white shark, but the story was originally inspired by several attacks off the coast of New Jersey by a bull shark. When you think of a killer shark, you'd probably picture a great white, but the bull shark is actually considered the most dangerous shark to humans with a powerful bite force of 1,350psi. But although there have been 121 bull shark attacks in total to date, only 25 of these have been fatal. This is nothing compared to how many sharks humans kill in just one year—a whopping 100 million. You have a one in a million chance of being bitten by a bull shark. You are actually more likely to get killed by a cow.

Fun Fact
Bull sharks are viviparous. This means they give birth to live young instead of laying eggs.

© Walter Geiersperger/Getty

Did you know...
Their jaws are made up of 350 teeth: 50 rows of about seven teeth each.

They can reach speeds of up to 25 mph.

BULL SHARK FACT FILE

CLASS
FISH

GROUP NAME
SCHOOL, SHOAL

TERRITORY
COASTAL WATERS WORLDWIDE

AVERAGE LIFE SPAN
UP TO 24 YEARS

DIET
CARNIVORE
FISH, MARINE MAMMALS, CRUSTACEANS, BIRDS, AND TURTLES

Bull sharks have poor vision, so they rely on their sense of smell to hunt.

HOW BIG!

Did you know...
Bull sharks get their name from their short snout, which they often use to headbutt their prey.

FEELING FRESH

Most sharks need salt water to survive, but bull sharks can thrive in fresh water for long periods of time. This is because their bodies are specially adapted to control the salt-to-water ratio. Their kidneys recycle the salt, and glands in their tails help retain the salt.

How to draw... a bull shark

1. BODY: Draw an eye shape, like this.

2. BELLY: Draw a straight line across the middle of the body shape.

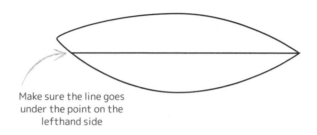

Make sure the line goes under the point on the lefthand side

3. TAIL: Create a boomerang-shaped tail on the righthand side of the body.

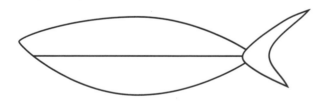

4. FINS: What's a shark without the famous shark fin that glides through the water? Add this at the top of the body. Then draw a smaller one underneath on the tummy line.

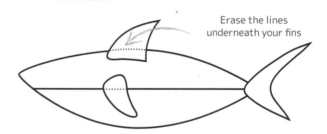

Erase the lines underneath your fins

5. FACE: Will your shark be fierce or kind? We've gone for a smiley face, but you can easily add some big, sharp teeth! Add an eye and three curved lines for the gills.

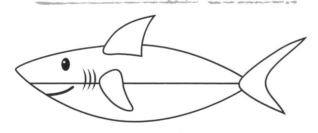

6. TWO TONE: Use a pale gray or blue for the belly of the shark, and a darker shade for the top and fins.

MORAY EEL

THESE SLIMY, SNAKE-LIKE FISH HAVE AN UNFAIR REPUTATION

You wouldn't think they were fish just by looking at them, but they are! Moray eels may look like snakes with slimy skin and sharp teeth, but these beautiful creatures are not aggressive unless threatened. Their skin is a layer of mucus for their own protection. Divers can find them hiding in rocks and crevices and, if they're lucky, might catch a glimpse of one gracefully undulating through the water. There are 200 species and the biggest of these is the giant moray, which can reach up to 9.8 feet and weighs 66 pounds. Morays have two sets of jaws; the first grabs hold of their prey to stop it escaping and the second then propels itself forward to bite.

©Hal Beral/Getty

©Reinhard Dirscherl/Alamy

Did you know...

Moray eels can be seen at "cleaning stations," where shrimp remove dead skin and parasites from their bodies.

Moray eels have poor vision and rely on their sense of smell to hunt.

GREEN MORAY EEL

FACT FILE

CLASS
FISH

GROUP NAME
SWARM

TERRITORY
WESTERN ATLANTIC OCEAN

HOW BIG!

AVERAGE LIFE SPAN
10—30 YEARS

DIET
CARNIVORE
FISH, CRABS, SHRIMP, OCTOPUS, AND SQUID

The green moray eel is actually brown; the mucus covering its skin is what makes it appear green.

Fun Fact
Morays are nocturnal, so you may have to take a night dive to spot one.

? Did you know...
You may think they're being aggressive, but when they're opening and closing their mouths they're simply breathing.

TIED UP IN KNOTS
Moray eels might tie their tails into a knot to use as an anchor or paddle in an attempt to dislodge prey when they're hunting in a crevice. But that's not all their multifunctional tail can do! They may also use the knot to strangle or crush their prey.

How to draw... a moray eel

1. EGG SHAPE: Start with an oval-shaped head.

2. BODY: Draw a curved, thin body, starting and finishing at the back of the head.

3. FIN: Draw a fin that goes the whole length of the eel, underneath the body and head.

Erase the original head line here

4. DORSAL FIN: Now draw another shorter fin on the top of the body, like this.

5. FACE AND STRIPES: Finally, add two eyes and a mouth, and lots of striped lines to the fins.

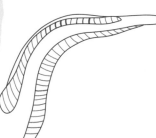

6. COLOR: Create an underwater night scene for your shy moray eel. Color it a nice shade of slime green!